HABITUAL HADITH FOR HUGE HEAVY HASANAT DURING SUCCESSFUL JIHADI RIBAT DOING ADHKAR AFTER SALAT

GREGORY HEARY

NO PAGE IN
YOUR BOOK OF
DEEDS ON THE
DAY OF TERROR
SHOULD BE
BLANK OR
WASTED WITH
SINS EVEN IF IT
IS ERASED BY
ALLAH DUE TO
REPENTANCE.

بِسْمِ اللهِ الرَّحْمٰنِ الرَّحِيْمِ

Say 1 time after the Athan:

اَللّٰهُمَّ رَبَّ هَذِهِ الدَّعوَةِ التَّامَّةِ، وَالصَّلَاةِ القَائِمَةِ، آتِ مُحَمَّدَانِ الوَسِيلَةَ وَالفَضِيلَةَ، وَابعَثهُ مَقَامًا مَّحمُودَانِ الَّذِي وَعَدتَهُ

Allahumma Rabba hadhi hid da'watit tammah was salatil qa-imah ati Muhammadanil wasilata wal fadilah, wab 'ath hu maqamam mahmuda nil-ladhi wa'adtahu

O Allah, Lord of this perfect call and owner of this prayer to be performed, grant Muḥammad ﷺ the intercession and favor, and raise him to the honored station You have promised him.

Narrated Jabir bin `Abdullah: Allah's Messenger (ﷺ) said,

"Whoever after listening to the Adhan says, 'Allahumma Rabba hadhihi-dda`watit-tammah, was-salatil qa'imah, ati Muhammadan al-wasilata wal-fadilah, wa b`ath-hu maqaman mahmudan-il-ladhi wa`adtahu' [O Allah! Lord of this perfect call (perfect by not ascribing partners to You) and of the regular prayer which is going to be established, give Muhammad the right of intercession and illustriousness, and resurrect him to the best and the highest place in Paradise that You promised him (of)], then my intercession for him will be allowed on the Day of Resurrection".

Sahih Bukhari 614

This book is a compilation of some strongly recommended Sunnah adhkar consisting of Dua, Ayat and Dhikr to be said after Salat meant to be convenient for English language Muslims displaying the Arabic, English Transliteration and English with the hadith included and sources cited. The goal is to make the prophetic post-Salat worship easier and habitual and to encourage the blessed act of Ribat. Yet first we started with the dua after Athan prior to the start of the Salat because of the priority of the blessed call and answering it first before we think about doing anything else after Salat. For which to properly respect the call we should be in our prayer spot before it is called, rather than answering it late. Are you preparing or just complying?

Many Muslims pray for the return of the days of violent prophetically ordained Jihadi conquest of the Kuffar. Yet many of us cannot even properly guard any of their five daily Salat let alone worship during it where, how, when, and why Allah deserves to be worshipped; if performed superficially. Hence for Muslim rulers to whom obedience is the Wajib Fard Sunnah they have few soldiers to even recruit for Jihad upon the prophetic method. For when we have 1% of the men who showed to Jumuah also show up to Fajr, what type of army can be raised to defend the blessed Ummah of heros? How can we even go further to defend the word of Allah by going on the offensive against the spiritual offenders regarding Allah's religion? Through prophetic footsteps following the tracks of the Sahabah by excelling in every aspect of

life training for the day we may meet our
enemy in battle whether from jinn or
humans preparing ourselves with
Tawheed, Iman and Taqwa by doing great
sincere deeds on a daily routine basis
years in advance. That is how the Jihadi
armies are created. And where are the
Jihadi bases located? In the purifying
hearts wet with tears of Tauba and sweat
from striving to do good and enjoining it
while avoiding evil and forbidding it. Yet
where do such hearts get the fuel needed
for such an excellent daily mission? Not
purely from Salat itself, for even the
munafiqeen during the prophet's time
complied 5 times a day in the masjid
Nabawi. It is achieved by what we do
after the Salat in between them. What I
refer to is the Adhkar, Dhikr, Dua and
Ribat; of which many fail in all categories
particularly Ribat after Salat. So I compile

this book hoping to help the Jihadis of the Ummah guard themselves and their families from the fire, whether they are human or jinn, male or female. For Ribat after Salat is a key ingredient of Jihadi training that counts as Jihad that can be done by every Salat performer on a daily basis, even the woman praying in her home. I believe such peaceful daily Ribat properly executed is a main ingredient of a Jihadi society that is missing worldwide in the blessed Ummah of Muslims. It is a practice I have tried daily and then lost for years and was blessed to subsequently revive in my own life after struggle and refinement to an extent I hope Allah will bless and accept. Truly daily life is miserable without this Ribat of Salat, if only you would perform it as a habit to get closer to Allah, as Allah blesses all who sincerely strive doing Salat and Ribat.

As a disclaimer not every hadith about Ribat is about the Ribat after Salat, as Ribat is also used to describe the military guarding the Muslim frontier borders. Yet for women who typically are not in the military, just as Hajj Mabrur is Jihad for them, Ribat after Salat is in fact a type of Jihad as are many peaceful non-military actions whether it be Ruqya, Dawah or even self-purification like Tazkiyyah or plain but divinely enjoyed Taubah repentance on our journey to the grave. Peaceful Jihad exists and you can do it, and must do it before halal military Jihad ever becomes an option for the Ummah.

From Zurah bin Ma'bad: "Abu Salih, said: 'I heard 'Uthman bin 'Affan say: I heard the Messenger of Allah (ﷺ) say:

Ribat (guarding) for one day in the cause of Allah is better in rank than a thousand days spent within the residence.'"

Sunan an-Nasa'i 3169 Sahih

While this hadith is classically reserved for the merits of military members, if closely analyzed "the cause of Allah" is what makes something better than 1,000 days in the residence. And just as spending Laylatul-Qadr in the residence in ibada is better than a regular worldly related residential day then it seems Ribat after Salat is likewise better than ordinary days spent in the residence outside of this blessed ibada in the cause of Allah. Even though Ribat after Salat can be done within the residence too sometimes.

It was narrated from Abu Hurairah that the Messenger of Allah (ﷺ) said:

*"Shall I not tell you of that by means of which Allah erases sins and raises in status? Doing Wudu' properly even when it is inconvenient, taking a lot of steps to the Masjid, **and waiting for one Salah after another. That is the Ribat for you, that is the Ribat for you, that is the Ribat for you."***

Sunan an-Nasa'i 143 Sahih

It was narrated that Salman said "I heard the Messenger of Allah (ﷺ) say:

'Whoever guards Ribat in the cause of Allah for one day and one night, he will have (a reward) like that of fasting and praying Qiyam for a month. If he dies he will continue to receive reward for what he did, and he will be kept safe from Al-Fattan, and he will be given provision.'"

Sunan Nasai 3167 Sahih

While this hadith and others on Ribat, which I won't mention, can be potentially restricted in meaning to be limited to military Jihadis, I don't believe they can actually be fully restricted to exclude the rewards of Ribat after Salat from coming under these rewards of military Ribat when we have clear hadith about Ribat after Salat being called/labeled Ribat. Why not? What is the evidence that one doing this peaceful Jihad of Ribat after Salat can qualify for rewards that the soldier guarding a military border can get?

Abu Huraira reported the Prophet (ﷺ) said,

"Allah says: 'I am just as My slave thinks I am, (i.e. I am able to do for him what he thinks I can do for him) and I am with him if He remembers Me. If he remembers Me in

himself, I too, remember him in Myself; and if he remembers Me in a group of people, I remember him in a group that is better than they; and if he comes one span nearer to Me, I go one cubit nearer to him; and if he comes one cubit nearer to Me, I go a distance of two outstretched arms nearer to him; and if he comes to Me walking, I go to him running.' "

Sahih al-Bukhari 7405

So, there is a real possibility for the rewards of Jihadi military Ribat to apply to the Ribat after Salat based on Hadith and the Quran and Allah being more generous than even the Quran and Hadith implies to our limited knowledge of them. For Allah can reward anyone greater than any listed reward in any information ever sent to earth for any deed Allah is pleased with. Also there are creatures who want to wage military Jihad but are incapable because of illness, gender, age, language, ability, or circumstances like being reverts, or being temporarily stuck in disbelieving countries without any current opportunity to join a Muslim Government's military to get the rewards of military Ribat they intend to achieve. Such creatures who truly sincerely desire that they could be a military Jihadi doing military Ribat and more, I hope qualify for their desired reward and more by doing what they can in preparation for the day of war by guarding Ribat after Salat daily or when they can as situations differ for every creature in every land. And even if I am wrong such an error may be rewarded as such anyways because Allah is more generous than all slaves' expectations. So even if some Scholars say it doesn't count and this understanding is a distorted way of seeking hasanat that can't be got that way, they will admit they still don't know what Allah will weigh this good deeds as.

Lastly and Firstly it is Allah we seek to reward us for Ribat after Salat, and this deed is a reward in itself. Even if we got zero reward for it in the afterlife, in this life such "Ribat" is a warship of worship we dare not abandon if we can stay upon it. We may drown without this worship just as we live better by doing it. So even if we're deluded into doing goodness that will get us less hasanat than expected we will never be disappointed in our Lord's reward for goodness. Still, we must prioritize correctly by doing the best deeds possible every day/night. Even if we didn't call this activity Ribat, as the Prophet did, then there are many hadith about this deed we love that are enough motivation for Allah's beloved. Also in a very real sense this type of Ribat is a type of guarding the prayer place whether it occurs in the important houses of Allah like the masjids, or the home; as their home is the best prayer place for women.

Abu Hurairah reported that the Messenger of Allah (ﷺ) said:

"Anyone amongst you who sat in a place of worship waiting for the prayer is in prayer and his ablution is not broken, the angels invoke blessing upon him (in these words): 'O Allah! Pardon him. O Allah! Have Mercy upon him.'"

Sahih Muslim 649k

Abu Huraira reported that Allah's Messenger (ﷺ) said:

"Verily, the mosques have pillars with whom the angels sit. If they are absent, the angels miss their presence. If they are sick, the angels visit them. If they are in need, the angels support them."

Musnad Aḥmad 9424 Hasan

Abu Darda reported that Allah's Messenger (ﷺ) said,

"The mosque is the home of every righteous person. Allah Almighty has guaranteed those who have their home in the mosques with the

*spirit, mercy, and safe passage over the bridge
of Hell unto the pleasure of Allah Almighty."*

Shu'ab al-Imān 2689 Hasan by Mundhiri

Anas reported that Allah's Messenger (ﷺ)
said,

 *"Allah will announce on the Day of
Resurrection: Where are my neighbors? Where
are my neighbors? The angels will say: Our
Lord, who is befitting to be your neighbor?
Allah will say: Where are those who filled the
mosques?"*

Musnad al-Ḥārith 126 Hasan by Albani

Anas bin Malik narrated that the
Messenger of Allah (ﷺ) said:

*"Whoever prays Fajr in congregation, then sits
remembering Allah until the sun has risen,
then he prays two Rak'ah (Duha Salat), then
for him is the reward like that of a Hajj and
Umrah." He said: "The Messenger of Allah
said: 'Complete, complete, complete.'"*

Jami` at-Tirmidhi 586 Hasan by Albani

Abu Umamah reported Allah's Messenger (ﷺ) said:

"If anyone goes out from his house after performing ablution for saying the prescribed prayer in congregation (in the mosque), his reward will be like that of one who goes for hajj pilgrimage after wearing ihram (worn by hajj pilgrims). And he who goes out to say the mid-morning (duha) prayer, and takes the trouble for this purpose, will take the reward like that of a person who performs umrah(minor pilgrimage). And a prayer followed by a prayer with no worldly talk during the gap between them will be recorded in Illiyyun(the book record of the pious deeds in heaven)."

Sunan Abi Dawud 558 Hasan

Abdullah bin Amr said:

"We performed the Maghrib (prayer) with the Messenger of Allah, then those who went back went back, and those who stayed, stayed. Then

the Messenger of Allah(ﷺ) came back in a hurry, out of breath, with his garment pulled up to his knees, and said: 'Be of good cheer, for your Lord has opened one of the gates of heaven and is boasting of you before the angels, saying: "Look at My slaves; they have fulfilled one obligatory duty and are awaiting another."

Sunan Ibn Majah 801 Sahih

Abu Hurairah reported that the Messenger of Allah (ﷺ) said:

"Everyone among you will be deemed to be occupied in Salat (prayer) constantly so long as Salat (the prayer) detains him (from worldly concerns), and nothing prevents him from returning to his family but Salat."

Riyad As-Salihin 1061 Sahih

Abu Huraira said the Prophet (ﷺ) said:

"When the words of Iqama are pronounced, do not come to (prayer) running, but go with

tranquility, and pray what you are in time for, and complete (what you have missed) for when one of you is preparing for prayer he is in fact engaged in prayer."

Sahih Muslim 602b

Salman reported The Prophet (ﷺ) said,

"Whoever performs ablution well in his home and then comes to the mosque, he is the guest of Allah, and it is a duty upon the Host to honor his guest."

Mu'jam al-Kabīr lil-Ṭabarānī 6139 Sahih

These hadith should be enough for you and motivation for the sincere strivers. So now if you are persuaded to do Ribat after Salat until the next Salat whether it be from a fard to a fard Salat or from Fajr to Duha/Ishraq Salat what are you supposed to do during that timeframe to please Allah most via the Sunnah? That varies on which Salat you are doing Ribat after. For example, after Fajr and Asr there are no Sunnah prayers although prayers like Taubah and Istikharra and Tahiyyatul-Masjid can be done after Fajr and Asr. So typically since Sunnah prayers are supposed to be done by men at home according to the Sunnah, and for sincerity, this generally makes Fajr and Asr the best times for men to do Ribat after Salat on a daily basis outside of Itikhaff in Ramadan. During these times after every Salat there are certain tasbeeh to say a certain number of times after Salat. During these times there are certain Quran verses to read after Salat. During these times there are certain other Adhkar and Dhikr. And during these times there are certain Dua to read, especially after Fajr and Asr, or Fajr and Maghrib depending on your scholastic opinion on what the evening is as referred to in the verses of the Quran 6:52-53,

وَلَا تَطْرُدِ ٱلَّذِينَ يَدْعُونَ رَبَّهُم بِٱلْغَدَوٰةِ وَٱلْعَشِيِّ يُرِيدُونَ وَجْهَهُ ۖ مَا عَلَيْكَ مِنْ حِسَابِهِم مِّن شَىْءٍ وَمَا مِنْ حِسَابِكَ عَلَيْهِم مِّن شَىْءٍ فَتَطْرُدَهُمْ فَتَكُونَ مِنَ ٱلظَّٰلِمِينَ

*And turn not away those who invoke their
Lord, morning and afternoon seeking His Face.
You are accountable for them in nothing, and
they are accountable for you in nothing, that
you may turn them away, and thus become of
the Zâlimûn(unjust).*

وَكَذَٰلِكَ فَتَنَّا بَعْضَهُم بِبَعْضٍ لِّيَقُولُوٓا۟ أَهَٰٓؤُلَآءِ مَنَّ ٱللَّهُ عَلَيْهِم مِّنۢ بَيْنِنَآ ۗ أَلَيْسَ ٱللَّهُ بِأَعْلَمَ بِٱلشَّٰكِرِينَ

*And thus We have tried some of them through
others that they might say, "Is it these whom
Allāh has favored among us?" Is not Allāh
most knowing of those who are grateful?*

To me it seems the opinion that after Asr
is the preferred time for the "evening"
duas is more correct because after
Maghrib we are commanded by hadith to
hasten to break our fast. Thus the
command to hasten to eat/drink after
fasting makes Ribat after Maghrib harder
while Ribat after Asr is always generally
easier throughout the year. Plus since the
angels shift change occurs at Fajr and Asr
there is another link joining Fajr and Asr

making it more likely that the Fajr and Evening duas could be better meant to be done at Asr time rather than Maghrib time though most times are good for dua. As a warning congregational dua after salat is an accursed innovative bida, just like rubbing your face after dua, or always raising your hands when doing the prescribed routine duas after salat, or using a dhikr or tasbeeh counter other than your fingers as the prophet commanded us to count dhikr on our fingers which testify on the Day of terrifying Resurrection for us. Also these dhikr, duas and ayat are to be read after Fard Salat prior to doing the Sunnah prayers. The rest of this is a handbook of some Sunnah ibada for Ribat after Salat that should become a routine for those doing this type of blessed ibada before choosing to fill the time with other ibada.

<u>Say 1 time Immediately after Tasleem:</u>

اللهُ أَكْبَر

Allah-hu Akbar

Allah is the greatest

Ibn Abbas said, we used to know that Allah's messenger had finished his prayer when we heard "Allahu Akbar".

Sahih Muslim 593

On the authority of Thawban that when the Messenger of Allah (ﷺ) finished his prayer. He begged forgiveness three times (by saying), **Say 3 times after Fard Salat:**

أَسْتَغْفِرُ اللهَ، أَسْتَغْفِرُ اللهَ،
أَسْتَغْفِرُ اللهَ

Astaghfirullah, Astaghfirullah, Astaghfirullah

I seek the forgiveness of Allah, I seek the forgiveness of Allah, I seek the forgiveness of Allah

Sahih Muslim 591

<u>Say 1 time after every Fard Salat:</u>

اللَّهُمَّ أَنْتَ السَّلاَمُ

وَمِنْكَ السَّلاَمُ

تَبَارَكْتَ يَا ذَا الْجَلاَلِ

وَالإِكْرَامِ

Allahumma antas-Salam wa minkas-salam, tabarakta ya Dhal-Jalaali wal-'Ikraam

O Allah You are the Flawless One, and from You comes peace and security. Blessed are You, Possessor of Majesty and Honour

Sahih Muslim 591

A'isha reported:

When the Messenger of Allah (ﷺ) pronounced salutation, after the salutation then it took him longer to say:

O Allah: Thou art Peace, and peace comes from Thee, blessed art Thou, Possessor of Glory and Honour; and in the narration of Ibn Numair the words are:" O Possessor of Glory and Honour."

Sahih Muslim 592

Say 1 time after every Fard Salat:

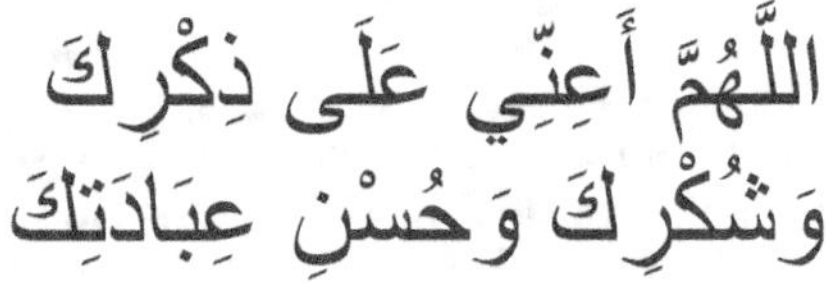

اللَّهُمَّ أَعِنِّي عَلَى ذِكْرِكَ وَشُكْرِكَ وَحُسْنِ عِبَادَتِكَ

Allahumma a'inni ala dhikrika, wa shukrika, wa husni 'ibadatika

O Allah! Help me to remember You, and to be thankful to You, and to worship You in the best manner.

Mu'adh bin Jabal reported Messenger of Allah (ﷺ) caught his hand and said:

By Allah, I love you, Mu'adh. I give some instruction to you. Never leave to recite this supplication after every (prescribed) prayer: "O Allah, help me in remembering You, in giving You thanks, and worshipping You well."

Sunan Abu Dawud 1522 Sahih

<u>**Say 1 time after every Fard Salat:**</u>

لاَ إِلَهَ إِلاَّ اللهُ وَحْدَهُ لاَ شَرِيكَ لَهُ لَهُ الْمُلْكُ وَلَهُ الْحَمْدُ وَهُوَ عَلَى كُلِّ شَىْءٍ قَدِيرٌ، لاَ حَوْلَ وَلاَ قُوَّةَ إِلاَّ بِاللهِ، لاَ إِلَهَ إِلاَّ اللهُ وَلاَ نَعْبُدُ إِلاَّ إِيَّاهُ لَهُ النِّعْمَةُ وَلَهُ الْفَضْلُ وَلَهُ

الثَّنَاءُ الْحَسَنُ، لاَ إِلَهَ إِلاَّ اللهُ مُخْلِصِينَ لَهُ الدِّينَ وَلَوْ كَرِهَ الْكَافِرُونَ

Laa ilaaha illallaahu wahdahu laa shareeka lahu, lahul mulku, wa lahul hamdu wa huwa 'alaa kulli shay-in qadeer. Laa hawla wa laa quwwata illaa billaah, laa ilaaha illallaahu, wa laa na'budu illaa iyyaah, lahun-ni'matu wa lahul fadhlu wa lahuth thanaa-ul hasan, laa ilaaha illallaahu mukhliseena lahud deena wa law karihal kaafiroon

None has the right to be worshiped but Allah alone, He has no partner, His is the dominion and His is the praise and He is Able to do all things. There is no power and no might except by Allah. None has the right to be worshiped but Allah, and we do not worship any other besides Him. His is grace, and His is bounty and to Him belongs the most excellent praise.

None has the right to be worshiped but Allah. (We are) sincere in making our religious devotion to Him, even though the disbelievers should disapprove.

Abu Zubair said:

"I heard 'Abd Allah bin al-Zubair saying on the pulpit: When the Prophet (ﷺ) finished the prayer, he used to say (at the end of the prayer): 'There is no God but Allah, Alone, Who has no partner, to Him belongs the Kingdom, to Him praise is due, and He is Omnipotent. There is no God but Allah to Whom we are sincere in devotion, even though the infidels should disapprove. To Him belongs wealth, to Him belongs grace and to Him is worthy accorded. There is no god but Allah to Whom we are sincere in devotion, even though infidels should disapprove.

Sunan Abu Dawood 1506 Sahih

<u>Say 33 time after every Fard Salat:</u>

سُبْحَانَ اللهِ – Subhan'Allah –

Glory be to Allah

<u>Say 33 time after every Fard Salat:</u>

Tahmid: الْحَمْدُ لِلهِ – Alhamdulillah –
Praise be to Allah

<u>Say 33 time after every Fard Salat:</u>

Takbir: اللهُ أَكْبَرُ – Allahu'Akbar –
Allah is the Most Great

<u>Say 1 time after every Fard Salat:</u>

Tahlil: لَا إِلَهَ إِلاَّ اللهُ –

La ilaaha illallah –

There is none worthy of worship except Allah

Abu Huraira reported he heard Allah's Messenger (ﷺ) as saying:

"If anyone extols Allah after every prayer thirty-three times, and praises Allah thirty-three times, and declares His Greatness thirty-three times, ninety-nine times in all, and says to complete a hundred:" There is no god but Allah, having no partner with Him, to Him belongs sovereignty and to Him is praise due, and He is Potent over everything," his sins will be forgiven even If these are as abundant as the foam of the sea."

Sahih Muslim 597

Say 3 times after Fajr and Evening Salat

$$ أَعُوْذُ بِكَلِمَاتِ اللهِ التَّامَّةِ مِنْ كُلِّ شَيْطَانٍ وَهَامَّةٍ وَمِنْ كُلِّ عَيْنٍ لَامَّةٍ $$

A'ooudhu bi kalimaat-illaahit-taammati min kulli shaytaanin wa haammah, wa min kulli ʿaynin laammah

O Allah! I seek Refuge with Your Perfect Words from every devil and from poisonous pests and from every evil, harmful, envious eye.' "

Narrated Ibn ʿAbbas: The Prophet (ﷺ) used to seek Refuge with Allah for Al-Hasan and Al-Husain and say: "Your forefather (i.e. Abraham) used to seek Refuge with Allah for Ishmael and Isaac by reciting the following: 'O Allah! I seek Refuge with Your Perfect Words from every devil and from poisonous pests and from every evil, harmful, envious eye.' "

Sahih Bukhari 3371

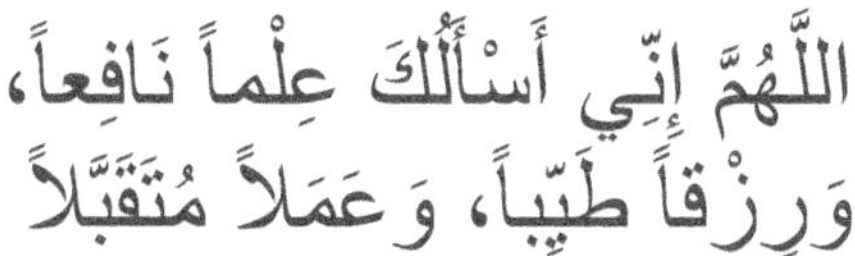

اللَّهُمَّ إِنِّي أَسْأَلُكَ عِلْماً نَافِعاً،
وَرِزْقاً طَيِّباً، وَعَمَلاً مُتَقَبَّلاً

Allahumma innee as-aluka 'ilman nafi'an, wa rizqan tayyiban, wa 'amalan mutaqabbalan

O Allah, I ask You for beneficial knowledge, goodly provision and acceptable deeds.

Umm Salamah said when the Prophet (ﷺ) performed the Subh (Fajr), while he said the Salam, he would say:

'Allahumma inni as'aluka 'ilman nafi'an, wa rizqan tayyiban, wa 'amalan mutaqabbalan (O Allah, I ask You for beneficial knowledge, goodly provision and acceptable deeds).'"

Sunan Ibn Majah 925 Sahih

اللَّهُ لَا إِلٰهَ إِلَّا هُوَ الْحَيُّ الْقَيُّومُ لَا تَأْخُذُهُ سِنَةٌ وَلَا نَوْمٌ لَّهُ مَا فِي السَّمَاوَاتِ وَمَا فِي الْأَرْضِ مَن ذَا الَّذِي يَشْفَعُ عِندَهُ إِلَّا بِإِذْنِه يَعْلَمُ مَا بَيْنَ أَيْدِيهِمْ وَمَا خَلْفَهُمْ وَلَا يُحِيطُونَ بِشَيْءٍ مِّنْ عِلْمِهِ إِلَّا بِمَا شَاءَ وَسِعَ كُرْسِيُّهُ السَّمَاوَاتِ وَالْأَرْضَ وَلَا يَئُودُهُ حِفْظُهُمَا وَهُوَ الْعَلِيُّ الْعَظِيمُ

Allahu laaa ilaaha illaa huwal haiyul qai-yoom; laa taakhuzuhoo sinatunw wa laa nawm; lahoo maa fissamaawaati wa maa fil ard; man zallazee yashfa'u indahooo illaa be iznih; ya'lamu maa

*baina aideehim wa maa khalfahum; wa
laa yuheetoona beshai 'immin 'ilmihee
illa be maa shaaaa; wasi'a kursiyyuhus
samaa waati wal arda wa la ya'ooduho
hifzuhumaa; wa huwal aliyyul 'adheem*

Allāh - there is no deity except Him, the
Ever-Living, the Self-Sustaining. Neither
drowsiness overtakes Him nor sleep. To
Him belongs whatever is in the heavens
and whatever is on the earth. Who is it
that can intercede with Him except by
His permission? He knows what is
before them and what will be after them,
and they encompass not a thing of His
knowledge except for what He wills. His
Kursī extends over the heavens and the
earth, and their preservation tires Him
not. And He is the Most High, the Most
Great.

On the authority of Abu Umamah who
narrated that the Prophet (ﷺ) said:

"Whoever recites Ayat ul-Kursi after each Obligatory Salah, nothing will be standing between him and Paradise except death."

Nasa'i in al-Kubra 9928 Sahih by Albani

Say 1 time after every Fard Salat

And/Or

Say 3 times after Fajr and Evening Salat:

قُلْ هُوَ ٱللَّهُ أَحَدٌ ٱللَّهُ ٱلصَّمَدُ

لَمْ يَلِدْ وَلَمْ يُولَدْ

وَلَمْ يَكُن لَّهُ كُفُوًا أَحَدٌ

Qul huwal laahu ahad Allah hus-samad Lam yalid wa lam yoolad Wa lam yakul-lahoo kufuwan ahad

Say, "He is Allah, [the] One, Allah, the Eternal Refuge. [the Self-Sufficient

Master, Whom all creatures need, (He neither eats nor drinks)] He neither begets nor is born, And there is none co-equal or comparable unto Him."

<u>Say 1 time after every Fard Salat:</u>

And/Or

<u>Say 3 times after Fajr and Evening Salat:</u>

قُلْ أَعُوذُ بِرَبِّ ٱلْفَلَقِ

مِن شَرِّ مَا خَلَقَ

وَمِن شَرِّ غَاسِقٍ إِذَا وَقَبَ

وَمِن شَرِّ ٱلنَّفَّاثَٰتِ فِي ٱلْعُقَدِ

وَمِن شَرِّ حَاسِدٍ إِذَا حَسَدَ

Qul a'oodhu bi rabbil-falaq Min sharri maa khalaq Wa min sharri ghaasiqin

izaa waqab Wa min sharrin-naffaa-
saati fil 'uqad Wa min sharri haasidin
izaa hasad

Say, "I seek refuge in the Lord of
daybreak. From the evil of that which
He created. And from the evil of
darkness when it settles. And from the
evil of those who practice witchcraft
when they blow in the knots. And from
the evil of an envier when he envies."

Say 1 time after every Fard Salat:

And/Or

Say 3 times after Fajr and Evening Salat:

قُلْ أَعُوذُ بِرَبِّ ٱلنَّاسِ
مَلِكِ ٱلنَّاسِ إِلَهِ ٱلنَّاسِ

مِن شَرِّ ٱلْوَسْوَاسِ ٱلْخَنَّاسِ
ٱلَّذِي يُوَسْوِسُ فِي صُدُورِ ٱ
لنَّاسِ مِنَ ٱلْجِنَّةِ وَٱلنَّاسِ

Qul a'oodhu birabbin naas Malikin naas Ilaahin naas Min sharril waswaasil khannaas Alladhee yuwaswisu fee sudoorin naas Minal jinnati wannaas

Say, "I seek refuge in the Lord of mankind, The King of mankind - The God of mankind, From the evil of the whisperer (devil who whispers evil in the hearts of men) who withdraws (from his whispering in one's heart after one remembers Allâh). Who whispers [evil] into the breasts of mankind From among the jinn and mankind."

Narrated 'Uqbah bin 'Amir:

"The Messenger of Allah (ﷺ) ordered me to recite Al-Mu'awwidhatain at the end of every Salat."

Jami Tirmidhi 2903 Hasan

Abdullah ibn Khubayb reported: The Messenger of Allah said,

"Speak." I said, "What should I say?" The Prophet said, "Say, 'He is Allah, the One,' (112) and the two chapters of refuge, al-Falaq(113) and al-Nas(114), every evening and morning three times. They will be enough for you against everything."

Source: Sunan al-Tirmidhī 3575

<u>Say 10 times after Fajr and Evening Salat,</u> and say 100 times during the whole day.

لاَ إِلَهَ إِلاَّ اللَّهُ وَحْدَهُ لاَ شَرِيكَ لَهُ لَهُ الْمُلْكُ وَلَهُ الْحَمْدُ يُحْيِي وَيُمِيتُ وَهُوَ عَلَى كُلِّ شَيْءٍ قَدِيرٌ

La Ilaha il-lallah wahdahu la shareeka
lahu, lahu mulku wa lahu hamdu yuhyi
wa yumeetu wa huwa ala kulli shayin
Qadir.

There is none worthy of worship except
Allaah alone, with no partner or
associate. His is the Dominion, to Him be
all praise, He gives life and causes death,
and He is powerful over all things.

Abu Dharr narrated that The Messenger of
Allah (ﷺ) said:

"Whoever says at the end of every Fajr
prayer, while his feet are still folded,
before speaking: 'None has the right to be
worshipped but Allah, Alone without
partner, to Him belongs all that exists, and
to Him is the praise, He gives life and
causes death, and He is powerful over all
things, (Lā ilāha illallāh, waḥdahu lā
sharīka lahu, lahul-mulku wa lahul-
ḥamdu, yuḥyī wa yumītu, wa huwa `alā
kulli shay'in qadīr)' ten times, then ten

good deeds shall be written for him, ten evil deeds shall be wiped away from him, ten degrees shall be raised up for him, and he shall be in security all that day from every disliked thing, and he shall be in protection from Shaitan, and no sin will meet him or destroy him that day, except for associating partners with Allah."

Jami Tirmidhi 3474 Hasan

Narrated Abu Huraira Allah's Messenger (ﷺ) said,

"If one says 100 times in one day: "None has the right to be worshipped but Allah, the Alone Who has no partners, to Him belongs Dominion and to Him belong all the Praises, and He has power over all things", one will get the reward of manumitting ten slaves, and one-hundred good deeds will be written in his account, and one-hundred bad deeds will be wiped off or erased from his account, and on that day he will be protected from the morning

till evening from Satan, and nobody will
be superior to him except one who has
done more than that which he has done."

Sahih al-Bukhari 3293

Say 1 time after Fajr Salat:

أَصْبَحْنَا وَأَصْبَحَ الْمُلْكُ لله وَالْحَمْدُ
لله ، لَا إِلَهَ إِلَّا اللهُ وَحْدَهُ لَا شَرِيكَ
لَهُ ، لَهُ الْمُلْكُ وَلَهُ الْحَمْدُ وَهُوَ
عَلَى كُلِّ شَيْءٍ قَدِيرٌ ، رَبِّ أَسْأَلُكَ
خَيْرَ مَا فِي هَذَا الْيَوْمِ وَخَيْرَ مَا
بَعْدَهُ ، وَأَعُوذُ بِكَ مِنْ شَرِّ مَا فِي
هَذَا الْيَوْمِ وَشَرِّ مَا بَعْدَهُ ، رَبِّ
أَعُوذُ بِكَ مِنَ الْكَسَلِ ، وَسُوءِ
الْكِبَرِ ، رَبِّ أَعُوذُ بِكَ مِنْ عَذَابٍ
فِي النَّارِ وَعَذَابٍ فِي الْقَبْرِ

Asbahna wa asbanhal mulku lilaahi wal
hamdulillahi, la ilaha il-lallah wahdhu la
shareeka lahu, lahu mulku wa lahu
hamdu wa huwa ala kulli shayin Qadir,
rabi asaluka khaiyra ma fee hadha
yawmi wa khaiyra ma baadahu wa
audhgu bika min sharee ma fee hadha
yawmi wa sharee ma badahu rabbi
audhu bika minal-kasali wa suuei kibari
rabbi audhu bika min adaabi fee Nari wa
adaabi fee Qabri

"We have entered upon the morning and
and the dominion belongs to Allah, all
the praise is for Allah, there is nothing
worthy of worship except for Allah, He is
alone having no partner, to Him belongs
the dominion and to Him belongs the
praise and He is Able to do all things.
My Lord, I ask you for the good that is in
this day and the good that will come after
it, and I seek refuge in You from the evil
in this day and the evil that will come
after it, My Lord I seek refuge in You
from laziness and the hardships of old

age , and I seek refuge in Your from the punishment of the Hellfire and the punishment in the grave."

The wording of the same dua above to be recited <u>1 time after the evening Salat is:</u>

أَمْسَيْنَا وَأَمْسَى الْمُلْكُ لِلّهِ، وَالْحَمْدُ لِلّهِ، لا إِلَهَ إِلاَّ اللهُ وَحْدَهُ لا شَرِيكَ لَهُ، لَهُ الْمُلْكُ وَلَهُ الْحَمْدُ وَهُوَ عَلَى كُلِّ شَيْءٍ قَدِيرٌ، رَبِّ أَسْأَلُكَ خَيْرَ مَا فِي هَذِهِ اللَّيْلَةَ وَخَيْرَ مَا بَعْدَهَا، وَأَعُوذُ بِكَ مِنْ شَرِّ مَا فِي هَذِهِ اللَّيْلَةَ وَشَرِّ مَا بَعْدَهَا، رَبِّ أَعُوذُ بِكَ مِنَ الْكَسَلِ وَسُوءِ الْكِبَرِ، رَبِّ أَعُوذُ بِكَ مِنْ عَذَابٍ فِي النَّارِ وَعَذَابٍ فِي الْقَبْرِ

Abdullah bin Mas'ud reported that Allah's Messenger (ﷺ) used to supplicate:

" We entered upon (morning or evening)
and the whole Kingdom of Allah also
entered upon (morning or evening) and
praise is due to Allah. There is no god but
Allah, the One Who has no partner with
Him."

Hasan said that Zubaid reported to him
that he memorised it from Ibrahim in
these very words.

" His is the Sovereignty and Praise is due
to Him, and He is Potent over everything.
O Allah, I beg of Thee the good of this
night and I seek refuge in Thee from the
evil of this night and the evil which
follows it. O Allah, I seek refuge in Thee
from sloth, from the evil of vanity. O
Allah, I seek refuge in Thee from torment
in the Hell-Fire and from torment in the
grave."

Sahih Muslim 2723

Say <u>1 time</u> after the Fajr Salat:

اللَّهُمَّ بِكَ أَصْبَحْنَا وَبِكَ أَمْسَيْنَا وَبِكَ نَحْيَا وَبِكَ نَمُوتُ وَإِلَيْكَ النُّشُورُ

Allahumma bika asbahna; Wa'bika amsaiyna; Wa'bika nahya; Wa'bika namootu; Wa'ilay'kaal nushoor.

O Allah, by Your leave we have reached the morning and by Your leave we have reached the evening, by Your leave we live and die and unto You is our return.

Say 1 time after the Evening Salat:

اللَّهُمَّ بِكَ أَمْسَيْنَا وَبِكَ نَحْيَا وَبِكَ نَمُوتُ وَإِلَيْكَ النُّشُورُ

Allahumma bika amsaiyna; Wa'bika nahya; Wa'bika namootu; Wa'ilay'kaal nushoor.

O Allah, by Your leave we come to the evening, by Your leave we die, and to You are we returned."

Abu Hurairah reported The Prophet (ﷺ) used to say in the morning:

 O Allah, by Your leave we have reached the morning and by Your leave we have reached the evening, by Your leave we live and die and unto You is our return.

In the evening he would say: " O Allah, by your leave we come to the evening, by Your leave we die, and to You are we returned."

Sunan abu Dawood 5068 Sahih

Say <u>3 times after Fajr and Evening Salat.</u>

بِسْمِ اللهِ الَّذِي لَا يَضُرُّ مَعَ اسْمِهِ شَيْءٌ فِي الْأَرْضِ وَلَا فِي السَّمَاءِ ، وَهُوَ السَّمِيعُ الْعَلِيمُ

Bismillah hil'lazee la yadur'oo ma'aasmihi shai-oon fil-ardi wa'laa fis-samaa; Wa'hu'waas samee'ool aa'leem.

In the name of Allah with whose name nothing is harmed on earth nor in the heavens and He is The All-Seeing, The All-Knowing

Aban bin `Uthman said "I heard `Uthman bin `Affan saying: 'The Messenger of Allah (ﷺ) said:"There is no worshiper who says, in the morning of every day, and the evening of every night: 'In the Name of Allah, who with His Name, nothing in the earth or the heavens can cause harm, and He is the Hearing, the Knowing – three times, (except) nothing shall harm him." Aban had been stricken with a type of semi-paralysis, so a man began to look at him, so Aban said to him, "What are you looking at? Indeed the Hadith is as I reported it to you, but I did not say it one day, so Allah brought about His decree upon me."
Jami Tirmidhi 3388 Hasan

Say 3 times after Evening Salat.

أَعُوذُ بِكَلِمَاتِ اللهِ التَّامَّاتِ
مِنْ شَرِّ مَا خَلَق

A'udhu Bikalimatillahit-Tammati Min Sharri Ma Khalaq

"I take refuge in Allah's perfect words from the evil He has created."

Abu Hurairah narrated that the Messenger of Allah (ﷺ) said:

"Whoever says three times when he reaches the evening: 'I seek refuge in Allah's Perfect Words from the evil of what he created, (A`ūdhu bikalimātillāhit-tāmmāti min sharri mā khalaq)' no poisonous sting shall harm him that night." Suhail said: "So our family used to learn it and they used to say it every night. A girl among them was stung, and she did not feel any pain."

Jami Tirmidhi 3604b Sahih

Khaula bint Hakim Sulamiyya reported I heard Allah's Messenger (ﷺ) as saying:

When anyone arrives at a place, and then says:" I seek refuge in the Perfect Word of Allah from the evil of what He has created," nothing would harm him until he marches from that stopping place.

Sahih Muslim 2708a

Say <u>1 time</u> after Fajr and Evening Salat:

اللَّهُمَّ فَاطِرَ السَّماوَاتِ وَالْأَرْضِ عَالِمَ الْغَيْبِ وَالشَّهَادَةِ ، رَبَّ كُلِّ شَيْءٍ وَمَلِيكَهُ ، أَشْهَدُ أَنْ لَا إِلَهَ إِلَّا أَنْتَ ، أَعُوذُ بِكَ مِنْ شَرِّ نَفْسِي ، وَمِنْ شَرِّ الشَّيْطَانِ وَشِرْكِهِ ، وَأَنْ أَقْتَرِفَ عَلَى نَفْسِي سُوءاً ، أَوْ أَجُرَّهُ إِلَى مُسْلِمٍ

Allāhumma fāṭiras-samāwāti wal-arḍi, `ālimal-ghaibi wash-shahādati, lā ilāha

illā anta, rabba kulli shai'in wa
malīkahu, a`ūdhu bika min sharri nafsī
wa min sharrish-shaiṭāni wa sharakihi,
wa an aqtarifa `alā nafsī sū'an, aw
ajurrahu ilā muslim

"O Allah, Originator of the heavens and
the earth, Knower of the unseen and
evident, Lord of everything and its
Possessor, I bear witness that there is
none worthy of worship but You. I seek
refuge in You (O Allah) from the evil of
my soul and from the evil of the devil
and his helpers/shirk/plots. I seek refuge
in You (O Allah) from bringing evil upon
my soul and from harming any Muslim."

Abu Rashid Al-Hubrani said:

"I came to `Abdullah bin `Amr and said to
him: 'Report something to me that you
heard from the Messenger of Allah (ﷺ).' So
he set forth before me a scroll and said:
'This is what the Messenger of Allah (ﷺ)
wrote for me.'" He said: "So I looked in it

and found in it: 'Indeed, Abu Bakr As-Siddiq, may Allah be pleased with him, said: "O Messenger of Allah, teach me what to say at morning and afternoon."

He said: "O Abu Bakr, say: 'O Allah, Creator of the heavens and the earth, Knower of the unseen and the seen, there is none worthy of worship except You, Lord of everything and its Owner, I seek refuge in You from the evil of my soul and from the evil of Shaitan and his Shirk, or that I should do some evil to myself or bring it upon a Muslim.'"

Jami Tirmidhi 3529

Say <u>1 time</u> after Fajr and Evening Salat:

اللَّهُمَّ أَنْتَ رَبِّي لَّا إِلَهَ إِلَّا أَنْتَ ، خَلَقْتَنِي وَأَنَا عَبْدُكَ ، وَأَنَا عَلَى عَهْدِكَ وَوَعْدِكَ مَا اسْتَطَعْتُ ،

أَعُوذُ بِكَ مِنْ شَرِّ مَا صَنَعْتُ ،
أَبُوءُ لَكَ بِنِعْمَتِكَ عَلَيَّ ، وَأَبُوءُ
لَكَ بِذَنْبِي فَاغْفِرْ لِي فَإِنَّهُ لَا يَغْفِرُ
الذُّنُوبَ إِلَّا أَنْتَ

Allaahumma Anta Rabbee laa ilaaha
illaa Anta, Khalaqtanee wa ana `abduka,
wa ana `alaa `ahdika wa wa`dika
mastaṭa`tu. A`oodhu bika min sharri maa
ṣana`tu. Aboo ulaka bini`matika `alayy,
wa aboo ulaka bidhanbee faghfirlee fa
innahoo laa yaghfirudh dhunooba illaa
Anta.

"O Allah, You are my Lord, there is none
worthy of worship but You. You created
me and I am Your slave. I am upon Your
covenant and Your promise to the best of
my ability. I seek Your Protection from
the evil that I have done. I acknowledge
Your blessings upon me, and I

acknowledge my sins. So forgive me, for no one forgive sins but You."

Narrated Shaddad bin Aus:

The Prophet (ﷺ) said "The most superior way of asking for forgiveness from Allah is: O Allah, You are my Lord, there is none worthy of worship except You. You have created me, and I am Your servant, and I am faithful to Your covenant and promise as much as I can. I seek refuge in You from the evil of what I have done. I acknowledge Your blessings upon me, and I admit my sins. So forgive me, for none forgives sins except You.

The Prophet (ﷺ) added. "If somebody recites it during the day with firm faith in it, and dies on the same day before the evening, he will be from the people of Paradise; and if somebody recites it at night with firm faith in it, and dies before the morning, he will be from the people of Paradise."

Sahih Bukhari 6306

اللَّهُمَّ إِنِّي أَسْأَلُكَ الْعَافِيَة فِي الدُّنْيَا وَالْآخِرَةِ. اللَّهُمَّ إِنِّي أَسْأَلُكَ الْعَفْوَ وَالْعَافِيَة فِي دِينِي وَدُنْيَايَ ، وَأَهْلِي وَمَالِي. اللَّهُمَّ اسْتُرْ عَوْرَاتِي ، وَآمِنْ رَوْعَاتِي. اللَّهُمَّ احْفَظْنِي مِنْ بَيْنِ يَدَيَّ وَمِنْ خَلْفِي ، وَعَنْ يَمِينِي وَعَنْ شِمَالِي ، وَمِنْ فَوْقِي ، وَأَعُوذُ بِعَظَمَتِكَ أَنْ أُغْتَالَ مِنْ تَحْتِي

Allaahumma innee as-alukal 'aafiyah fid-dunyaa wal-aakhirah. Allaahumma innee as-alukal 'afwa wal 'aafiyah fee deenee wa dunyaaya wa ahlee wa maalee. Allaahummastur 'awraatee, wa aamin raw'aatee. Allaahummahfaḍhnee

min bayni yadayya, wa min khalfee, wa
'an yameenee wa 'an shimaalee, wa min
fawqee, wa a'oodhu bi 'aḍhamatika an
ughtaala min taḥtee

"O Allah, I ask You for well-being in this
world and the Next. O Allah, I ask You
for forgiveness and well-being in my
religion, in this world, in my family and
my property. O Allah, conceal my faults
and calm my fears/that which causes my
worry. O Allah, give me protection from
in front of me and behind me, from my
right and my left, and from above me. I
seek refuge by Your might from being
suddenly struck from beneath me."

Narrated Abdullah ibn Umar:

The Messenger of Allah (ﷺ) never failed to
utter these supplications in the evening
and in the morning: O Allah, I ask Thee
for security in this world and in the
Hereafter: O Allah! I ask Thee for
forgiveness and security in my religion

and my worldly affairs, in my family and
my property; O Allah! Conceal my fault or
faults (according to Uthman's version),
and keep me safe from the things which I
fear; O Allah! Guard me in front of me and
behind me, on my right hand and on my
left, and from above me: and I seek in Thy
greatness from receiving unexpected harm
from below me."

Sunan Abu Dawood 5074 Sahih

Say <u>1 time</u> after Fajr and Evening Salat:

يَا حَيُّ يَا قَيُّومُ ، بِرَحْمَتِكَ
أَسْتَغِيثُ ، أَصْلِحْ لِي شَأْنِي
كُلَّهُ ، وَلَا تَكِلْنِي إِلَى نَفْسِي
طَرْفَةَ عَيْنٍ

Yaa Ḥayyu yaa Qayyoom, biraḥmatika
astagheeth, aṣliḥlee sha`nee kullahu, wa
laa takilnee ilaa nafsee ṭarfata 'aynin

"O Ever living One, O Self-Sustaining
All-Sustaining One, I seek assistance
through Your Mercy, rectify all of my
affairs for me, and do not leave me in
charge of my soul for even the blinking
of an eye."

Anas ibn Malik said: The Prophet said to
Fatimah: "What could prevent you from
listening to the advice I give you? You
should say when morning comes and
when evening comes: O Ever-Living, O
Self-Sustaining and All-Sustaining, by
Your mercy I seek help; rectify all my
affairs and do not leave me in charge of
my affairs even for the blink of an eye."

Nasaa'i in Kubra 6/147 Hasan by Albani

اللّٰهُمَّ عافِني في بَدَني ، اللّٰهُمَّ عافِني في سَمْعي ، اللّٰهُمَّ عافِني في بَصَري ، لا إِلٰهَ إلاَّ أَنْتَ

Allaahumma 'aafinee fee badanee, Allaahumma 'aafinee fee sam'ee, Allaahumma 'aafinee fee baṣaree, laa Ilaaha illaa Anta

"O Allah, make me healthy in my body. O Allah preserve for me my hearing. O Allah preserve for me my sight. There is none truly worthy of worship but You.

Say <u>3 times</u> after Fajr and Evening Salat:

اللّٰهُمَّ إِنّي أَعوذُبِكَ مِنَ الْكُفر ، وَالْفَقْر ، وَأَعوذُبِكَ مِنْ عَذابِ القَبْر ، لا إِلٰهَ إلاَّ أَنْتَ

**Allaahumma innee a'oodhu bika minal
kufri, wal faqri, wa a'oodhu bika min
'adhaabil qabri, laa Ilaaha illaa Anta.**

**O Allah I seek refuge in You from
disbelief and poverty and I seek refuge
in You from the punishment of the grave.
There is none truly worthy of worship
but You."**

Abdur Rahman ibn Abu Bakrah said that
he told his father: O my father! I hear you
supplicating every morning: "O Allah!
Grant me health in my body. O Allah!
Grant me good hearing. O Allah! Grant
me good eyesight. There is no god but
Thou." You repeat them three times in the
morning and three times in the evening.

He said: I heard the Messenger of Allah
(ﷺ) using these words as a supplication
and I like to follow his practice.

The transmitter, Abbas, said in this
version: And you say: "O Allah! I seek

refuge in Thee from infidelity and
poverty. O Allah! I seek refuge in Thee
from punishment in the grave. There is no
god but Thee". You repeat them three
times in the morning and three times in
the evening, and use them as a
supplication. I like to follow his practice.

Sunan Abu Dawood 5090 Sahih

Say <u>3 times</u> after Fajr and Evening Salat:

سُبْحَانَ اللهِ وَبِحَمْدِهِ ، عَدَدَ خَلْقِهِ ،
وَرِضَا نَفْسِهِ ، وَزِنَةَ عَرْشِه ،
ومِداد كَلِماته

**SubḥaanAllaahi wa biḥamdihee, 'adada
khalqihee, wa riḍaa nafsihee, wa zinata
'arshihee, wa midaada kalimaatihee**

**Perfection and all Praise belongs to
Allah, as many times as the number of
His creatures, in accordance with His
Good Pleasure, equal to the weight of
His Throne and equal to the ink that may**

be used in recording the words (for His Praise)]."

Juwairiya reported that Allah's Messenger (ﷺ) came out from (her apartment) in the morning as she was busy in observing her dawn prayer in her place of worship. He came back in the forenoon and she was still sitting there. He (the Prophet) said:

You have been in the same seat since I left you? She said: Yes. Thereupon Allah's Messenger (ﷺ) said: I recited four words three times after I left you and if these are to be weighed against what you have recited since morning these would outweigh them and (these words) are:" Glory be to Allah and praise is due to Him according to the number of His creation and according to the pleasure of His Self and according to the weight of His Throne and according to the ink (used in recording) words (for His Praise)."

Sahih Muslim 2726a

أَصْبَحْنَا عَلَى فِطْرَةِ الْإِسْلَامِ ، وَعَلَى كَلِمَةِ الْإِخْلَاصِ ، وَعَلَى دِينِ نَبِيِّنَا مُحَمَّدٍ صَلَّى اللهُ عَلَيهِ وَسَلَّمَ ، وَعَلَى مِلَّةِ أَبِينَا إِبْرَاهِيمَ ، حَنِيفاً مُسْلِماً وَمَا كَانَ مِنَ الْمُشْرِكِينَ

Aṣbaḥnaa 'alaa fiṭratil Islaami wa 'alaa kalimatil ikhlaaṣ, wa 'alaa deeni nabiyyinaa Muhammadin (ṣallallaahu 'alayhi wa sallama), wa 'alaa millati abeenaa Ibraaheema, ḥaneefan Musliman wa maa kaana minal mushrikeen.

"We have entered a new day upon the natural religion of Islam, the word of sincere devotion, the religion of our Prophet Muhammad (ﷺ), and the faith of our father Ibrahim. He was upright (in worshiping Allah) and a Muslim. He was not of those polytheists who worship others besides Allah."

Abdullāh bin ʿAbd al-Raḥman bin Abzá from his father

"The Prophet ﷺ used to say, 'In the morning and in the evening, we are upon the natural way of Islam, upon the statement of sincerity, upon the religion of our prophet Muhammad ﷺ, and upon the way of our father Ibrahim, who was upright and a Muslim, and he was not among the polytheists.'"

Musnad Ahmed 15363

Say <u>1 time</u> after Fajr Salat:

رَضِيْتُ بِاللهِ رَبَّاً وَبِالْإِسْلاَمِ دِيْناً
وَبِمُحَمَّدٍ صَلَّى اللَّهُ عَلَيْهِ وَسَلَّمَ نَبِيَّاً

Raḍeetu biLlaahi Rabban wa bil Islaami Deenan, wa bi Muḥammadin (ṣallallaahu 'alayhi wa sallama) nabiyyan

"I am pleased with Allah as my Lord, with Islam as my religion and with Muhammad as my Prophet."

Abu Sa'id al-Khudri reported: The Messenger of Allah said, "Whoever is pleased with Allah as a Lord, with Islam as a religion, and with Muhammad as a prophet, he must enter Paradise."

Sahih Muslim 1884

Say <u>1 time</u> after Fajr and Evening Salat:

اَللَّهُمَّ قِنِيْ شَرَّ نَفْسِيْ، وَاعْزِمْ لِيْ عَلَى أَرْشَدِ أَمْرِيْ اَللَّهُمَّ اغْفِرْ لِيْ مَا أَسْرَرْتُ وَمَا أَعْلَنْتُ، وَمَا أَخْطَأْتُ وَمَا عَمَدْتُ، وَمَا جَهِلْتُ.

Allaahumma qini sharra nafsi, wa'jim lee alaa arshadi amri, Allaahummaghfir lee maa as'rartu wa maa a'lantu wa maa akhta'tu wa maa amadtu wa maa jahiltu.

O Allah, keep me safe from the evil of my soul. Give me a strong will to do good in all things. O Allah, forgive me all that I have done openly and secretly, that which I have done willingly and unwillingly, and that which I have done in ignorance.

Husayn narrated to us; Shayban narrated to us; from Mansur; from Rib'i ibn Hirash; from Imran ibn Husayn or someone else:

That Husayn or Hasin came to the Messenger of Allah and said: "O Muhammad, 'Abd al-Muttalib was better for his people than you. He used to feed them liver and hump meat, while you are slaughtering them!" The Prophet said to him whatever Allah willed him to say, then he said to him: "What do you command me to say?" He replied: "Say: 'O Allah, protect me from the evil of my own soul, and determine for me the most rightly guided course in my affairs.'"

He said: Then the man went away and embraced Islam. After that he came back and said: "I came to you, and you told me: 'Say: O Allah, protect me from the evil of my own soul, and determine for me the most rightly guided course in my affairs.' What should I say now?" He said: "Say: 'O Allah, forgive me for what I have concealed and what I have made public, what I have done by mistake and what I have done deliberately, what I have known and what I have been ignorant of.'"

Musnad Ahmad 19992 Grade: Sahih

Say <u>100 times a day at any time</u>:

Subḥaan Allaahi wa biḥamdihi

Perfection and all Praise belongs to Allah

Narrated Abu Huraira:

Allah's Messenger (ﷺ) said, "Whoever says, 'Subhan Allah wa bihamdihi,' one hundred times a day, will be forgiven all his sins even if they were as much as the foam of the sea.

Sahih Bukhari 6405

Narrated Abu Huraira:

The Prophet (ﷺ) said, "There are two expressions which are very easy for the tongue to say, but they are very heavy in

the balance and are very dear to The
Beneficent (Allah), and they are,

'Subhan Allah Al- `Adheem
and
'Subhan Allah wa bihamdihi.'"
Sahih Bukhari 6406

Say <u>100 times a day</u> at any time:

أَسْتَغْفِرُ اللّٰهَ وَأَتُوبُ إِلَيْه

Astaghfirullaaha wa atoobu ilayhi

**"I seek Allah's forgiveness, and to Him
I repent."**

Al-Aghar al-Muzani reported: The
Messenger of Allah said, "Verily, there is
fog over my heart at times, so I seek the
forgiveness of Allah one hundred times in
a day."

Ṣaḥīḥ Muslim 2702

Shaykh Al-Albani (رحمه الله) said: "If someone is in a hurry after the (obligatory) prayer, they should not leave off the remembrance (after the salah), and (instead) he should say them whilst he is walking." [Fatawa Jeddah, 24]

The same applies to adhkar done at anytime, Allah says in the Quran 4:103,

فَإِذَا قَضَيْتُمُ الصَّلَاةَ فَاذْكُرُوا اللَّهَ قِيَامًا وَقُعُودًا وَعَلَىٰ جُنُوبِكُمْ

"When you have finished As-Salat (the prayer), remember Allah standing, sitting down, and (lying down) on your sides."

This handbook ends with a blessed promise from Allah in the Quran 29:69,

وَالَّذِينَ جَاهَدُوا فِينَا لَنَهْدِيَنَّهُمْ سُبُلَنَا ۚ وَإِنَّ اللَّهَ لَمَعَ الْمُحْسِنِينَ

As for those who strive hard for Us (Our Cause), We will surely guide them to Our Paths (Allâh's Salafi religion - Islâmic Monotheism). And verily, Allâh is with the Muhsinûn (good doers)."

NO PAGE IN
YOUR BOOK OF
DEEDS ON THE
DAY OF TERROR
SHOULD BE
BLANK OR
WASTED WITH
SINS EVEN IF IT
IS ERASED BY
ALLAH DUE TO
REPENTANCE.